WHY ASTEROID MINING COULD SAVE THE EARTH?
Hidden Treasures of the Cosmos

An Inside Look at the Science, Economics, Potential of Space Resources, Billion-Dollar Opportunities, and Humanity's Next Frontier

Scott W. Diego

Table of Contents

Introduction

Imagine a world where the search for resources stretches beyond our planet, a vision once confined to science fiction that is now edging toward reality. As Earth's resources continue to dwindle, humanity is forced to confront an uncomfortable truth: the materials that fuel our technology, infrastructure, and everyday lives are finite. Over centuries, we have extracted countless tons of metals, minerals, and rare elements from the Earth's crust, yet these resources are not boundless. The pressure on our planet's environment, combined with escalating demands from industries and technological advancements, has created an urgent need for alternative sources of essential materials. Enter the concept of asteroid mining, a revolutionary approach that seeks not only to alleviate our planet's resource depletion but to do so in a way that could propel us toward a sustainable and prosperous future.

Asteroids are more than remnants of cosmic debris scattered across space; they are vast reservoirs of precious metals and minerals, including elements such as nickel, cobalt, platinum, and even water ice. Unlike Earth's crust, which holds only a fraction of these materials, asteroids are rich with concentrated elements left largely untouched since the formation of the solar system. These celestial bodies, many of which orbit close to Earth, represent an untapped potential that could reshape industries, economies, and environmental strategies across the globe. The idea of mining asteroids might sound like the stuff of fantastical tales, yet technological advances in space exploration and resource extraction have brought this once-impossible dream within reach. The implications of accessing space resources go far beyond mere profit; asteroid mining could serve as a critical turning point in human history, allowing us to relieve the environmental strain on Earth while expanding our reach into the cosmos.

This book embarks on a journey to explore the practical and theoretical dimensions of asteroid mining. It delves into the science behind these mineral-rich objects, examining their formation and unique compositions, which make them valuable to our future. Through this journey, we encounter the engineering and logistical challenges that come with launching resource extraction into space, as well as the economic models that attempt to make this venture viable in the eyes of investors and governments alike. Alongside these insights, the book considers the ethical and legal implications of claiming resources from beyond our planet, raising questions about ownership, benefit sharing, and global impact. Ultimately, the exploration of asteroid mining is not only a tale of advanced technology and visionary ambitions but also a reflection of humanity's quest to balance growth and sustainability on an interplanetary scale.

Through this detailed analysis, the book invites readers to envision a future where humanity no longer solely relies on Earth's resources. Instead, we might look to the stars, embracing the possibilities that lie in the vast expanse of space. This shift in thinking brings with it an unprecedented potential to transform our industries, reimagine our economies, and, ultimately, secure a thriving existence for generations to come.

Chapter 1: The Rationale for Asteroid Mining

The Earth, with its deep oceans, dense forests, and sprawling landscapes, has long provided an abundant source of resources for human development. Over millennia, we have extracted metals, minerals, fossil fuels, and other materials to power civilizations, advance technology, and fuel economic growth. Yet, this constant extraction comes at a steep cost. Beneath the surface, our planet is facing a silent depletion, where the once plentiful reserves of critical elements such as cobalt, platinum, and rare earth minerals are steadily vanishing. This gradual exhaustion, while invisible to most, is triggering environmental pressures and economic shifts that ripple across the globe, pressing humanity to search beyond the boundaries of Earth for solutions.

As industries expand, especially in high-tech and renewable sectors, the demand for certain metals has surged to unprecedented levels. Metals like lithium and cobalt, essential for batteries and clean energy technology, are mined in vast quantities to support the shift toward sustainable energy sources. At the same time, precious metals like platinum and palladium, used extensively in electronics and catalytic converters, have become increasingly scarce. As these resources become harder to access, extraction efforts have pushed into sensitive ecosystems, often leaving scars on landscapes, contaminating water sources, and disrupting local communities. This environmental toll, combined with escalating resource scarcity, poses a dilemma: how can we continue to meet the demands of a growing population without exhausting the very materials that sustain our way of life?

The impact of resource depletion is acutely felt within modern society's economic and industrial frameworks. Industries reliant on rare metals, from smartphone manufacturers to electric vehicle producers, now face rising material costs and supply instability. As these metals become rarer, competition for access grows fierce, prompting political tensions and sparking discussions around resource nationalism. Countries rich in minerals may restrict exports to secure resources for domestic use, disrupting global supply chains and further driving up prices. For high-demand materials like lithium and rare earth elements, the implications are particularly stark, with nations vying to secure stable supply lines in an increasingly competitive market.

These pressures create not only economic strain but also expose vulnerabilities in modern infrastructure and technology. The transition to renewable energy, for example, depends heavily on metals like lithium and cobalt for energy storage and solar panels. Without a reliable supply, progress toward sustainable energy systems may stall, impeding efforts to combat climate change. Moreover, as the costs of these materials soar, it affects industries ranging from electronics to automotive, where manufacturing prices rise, ultimately impacting consumers.

This scarcity reveals a deeper fragility in our reliance on Earth's resources and prompts an urgent question: if our planet cannot indefinitely supply these materials, where will we turn next? The search for alternative sources becomes not just an option but a necessity, leading many to look toward the vast, untapped reservoirs of metals and minerals lying beyond Earth's gravitational pull. The idea of sourcing resources from space, once the realm of pure speculation, is gaining traction as a solution to these mounting challenges. As asteroid mining emerges as a potential answer to our resource woes, it signifies a transformative step that could change not only the way we source materials but also how we envision our relationship with the cosmos.

Asteroids, remnants of the early solar system, are far more than scattered space rocks; they are ancient vaults of valuable metals and minerals that offer a glimpse into the solar system's raw composition. Unlike Earth, where gravity has pulled heavier elements deep into the core over billions of years, many asteroids retain a high concentration of metals and minerals closer to their surfaces. These materials, untouched and preserved for eons, could provide an abundant source of elements essential for technological progress and industrial sustainability on Earth.

Among the precious resources in these celestial bodies, nickel, cobalt, iron, and platinum are of particular interest. Nickel and cobalt are fundamental to high-performance batteries, critical for everything from electric vehicles to renewable energy storage. Iron, though abundant on Earth, remains a foundational element for countless industries, from construction to manufacturing. Platinum, known for its catalytic properties, is highly sought after for use in electronics, medical equipment, and emissions-reducing technology. Rare earth elements, though present in small quantities on many asteroids, are invaluable due to their unique properties, making them essential components in advanced technologies such as smartphones, wind turbines, and satellite systems.

Asteroids are incredibly diverse in their composition. The specific types of asteroids, known as C-type, S-type, and M-type, each hold a different range of resources. C-type, or carbonaceous asteroids, often contain water in addition to organic compounds, which could prove invaluable for sustaining human life in space and creating rocket fuel. S-type, or silicaceous asteroids, contain a mix of metals and silicate rock, while M-type, or metallic asteroids, are known for their high concentrations of metals, including iron and nickel. This classification allows scientists to identify which asteroids might be the most resource-rich, guiding future exploration and mining missions toward the most promising targets.

What makes asteroids especially intriguing as resource depositories is the accessibility of these metals compared to Earth's reserves. On Earth, obtaining rare metals often requires drilling deep into the crust, which can be costly and environmentally destructive. Asteroids, in contrast, offer these metals much closer to the surface, in quantities that could dwarf what we currently mine on Earth. Some of these metals, such as those found on asteroid 16 Psyche, are believed to exist in massive deposits, remnants of failed planetary cores that have left dense, metal-rich bodies behind. This unique formation history means that the metals found on certain asteroids are both abundant and accessible, requiring only the technology to reach and extract them.

The significance of these asteroid-borne resources cannot be overstated. As Earth's supplies of these metals diminish, securing a new, potentially limitless source in space could revolutionize industries and stabilize the supply chains that underpin modern technology. Asteroids represent a new frontier not only in terms of exploration but also as a strategic reserve for materials essential to a sustainable, technologically advanced future on Earth. This abundance, if harnessed, could allow humanity to continue advancing without depleting our planet's resources, potentially transforming how we build, manufacture, and power the world.

Chapter 2: The Science of Asteroids and Their Composition

Asteroids are more than just cosmic leftovers drifting through space; they are diverse entities with distinct compositions that offer insights into the building blocks of the solar system. These differences in mineral makeup define the types of asteroids—C-type, S-type, and M-type—each with unique characteristics and potential resources. Understanding these types is essential, as they determine which asteroids are the most promising for future mining efforts.

C-type, or carbonaceous asteroids, are the most common, making up roughly 75% of the known asteroid population. These dark, carbon-rich bodies are found mainly in the outer regions of the asteroid belt and are distinguished by their high content of organic compounds and hydrated minerals. One of the most intriguing aspects of C-type asteroids is their water content, often in the form of ice, which could be harvested for life support and fuel in space. Additionally, they contain nitrogen, hydrogen, and ammonia, all of which could play crucial roles in supporting long-term human presence beyond Earth. This water potential makes C-type asteroids appealing targets for missions aiming to establish self-sufficient space infrastructure, as the water extracted could be converted into oxygen and hydrogen fuel.

S-type, or silicaceous asteroids, make up about 17% of the asteroid population and are predominantly located in the inner regions of the asteroid belt. They are composed primarily of silicate materials and nickel-iron, making them rich in metals useful for industry. While S-types generally contain less water than C-types, they offer higher concentrations of metals like iron, nickel, and magnesium, which are critical to manufacturing and construction. S-type asteroids can be particularly valuable as sources of metals that are often difficult and expensive to mine on Earth.

Because they are relatively closer to Earth compared to some other asteroid types, S-types are considered accessible for early mining missions.

M-type, or metallic asteroids, are rarer than C-types and S-types but potentially far more valuable. They are thought to have formed from the remnants of protoplanetary cores, where heavy elements were drawn inward, leaving dense concentrations of metals. These metallic asteroids, primarily composed of nickel and iron, often contain precious metals like platinum, gold, and iridium. M-types are of exceptional interest because of their high metal density, making them an ideal target for mining missions aimed at recovering large amounts of valuable resources. Some M-type asteroids, like 16 Psyche, are considered treasure troves, as they might contain more metal than has been mined on Earth throughout human history.

The differences among these types of asteroids are more than just scientific distinctions; they shape the possibilities for space mining strategies. While

C-type asteroids might be targeted for their water content to support life and fuel in space, S-types and M-types offer valuable metals for use in construction, technology, and potentially even for supporting future space-based economies. By understanding these compositions, scientists and space agencies can better plan missions, matching specific asteroid types with the needs of sustainable development and industrial expansion in space. Each type of asteroid presents unique resources that, if harvested efficiently, could fuel humanity's expansion beyond Earth, creating new pathways for economic and technological growth in the cosmos.

Asteroids are the ancient remnants of the early solar system, formed over 4.5 billion years ago during a period of intense gravitational upheaval. In this chaotic environment, dust and gas clumped together to create planetesimals, the building blocks of planets. Some of these planetesimals grew to form planets, while others were left fragmented, resulting in the diverse collection of asteroids we see today. Because of their unique origins, asteroids carry an assortment of elements, including metals and minerals that are rare on Earth. This is due to the fact that, unlike planets, many asteroids never developed cores, mantles, or crusts that would separate lighter and heavier elements. As a result, they remain as concentrated repositories of metals that, on Earth, are often deeply buried and difficult to access.

The resource wealth found in asteroids is tied to the varied conditions under which they formed. These primordial bodies contain metals and minerals that have remained virtually unchanged since the solar system's formation, making them highly valuable for mining. Elements like iron, nickel, cobalt, and platinum are found in some abundance on certain asteroids, and these metals are critical for modern technology, manufacturing, and clean energy solutions. In particular, metals such as platinum and palladium are rare on Earth, due to their heavy atomic structures that caused them to sink deep within Earth's core during planetary differentiation. However, in many asteroids, these metals are readily accessible, lying closer to the surface or within shallow layers, making them ideal targets for future resource extraction.

Among the most studied near-Earth asteroids are Bennu and Ryugu, both of which offer valuable insights into the composition and mining potential of space resources. Bennu, a carbon-rich asteroid, has a composition that suggests it holds water-bearing minerals, valuable for future space missions as both life support and potential fuel sources. Estimated to be worth around $700 million, Bennu is composed mainly of carbonaceous material but also holds iron and nickel. The OSIRIS-REx mission by NASA was sent to Bennu to collect samples, successfully bringing back fragments in 2023. The findings from Bennu have highlighted the potential for extracting both water and metals from similar carbonaceous asteroids, making Bennu a valuable case study in developing strategies for future mining operations.

Ryugu, another near-Earth asteroid, has also drawn considerable attention, especially from Japan's space agency, JAXA. Ryugu, like Bennu, contains water-bearing minerals, but it also has significant concentrations of nickel, cobalt, and iron, which are essential for industrial applications. The Hayabusa2 mission to Ryugu successfully collected samples in 2020, revealing a complex composition with organic materials and a range of metals. Ryugu's estimated resource value is around $80 billion, making it economically attractive for future exploration. What sets Ryugu apart is its accessibility, as experts believe that a mining operation could yield substantial returns after accounting for extraction costs. Ryugu exemplifies the potential for near-Earth asteroids to serve as resource reservoirs, especially when proximity and mineral wealth combine to make them viable targets for mining initiatives.

Perhaps the most extraordinary example of asteroid resource wealth is 16 Psyche, a massive M-type asteroid located in the asteroid belt between Mars and Jupiter. Unlike Bennu and Ryugu, 16 Psyche is thought to be the exposed metallic core of an early planetesimal that was stripped of its outer layers, leaving behind an enormous deposit of nickel, iron, and potentially precious metals like platinum and gold. Estimates place the value of 16 Psyche's resources in the range of $10,000 quadrillion, a staggering amount that surpasses the entire global economy. The metallic composition of Psyche suggests that it is unlike any other known asteroid, as it may provide a snapshot of planetary cores that are otherwise inaccessible. NASA's planned mission to Psyche will attempt to confirm its composition, offering insight not only into planetary formation but also into the feasibility of mining its abundant metals.

These case studies—Bennu, Ryugu, and 16 Psyche—demonstrate the incredible diversity and resource potential found in asteroids. Each one offers unique opportunities for understanding asteroid composition, advancing mining technology, and even supporting the creation of a space-based economy. Whether carbon-rich and close to Earth like Bennu, metal-laden and accessible like Ryugu, or a potential goldmine like 16 Psyche, these asteroids could represent the next step in humanity's journey to source essential resources without depleting our planet. In studying and potentially mining these ancient cosmic bodies, we are not only preserving Earth's resources but also paving the way for a new era in space exploration and industry.

Chapter 3: Legal and Ethical Considerations of Space Mining

As humanity inches closer to extracting resources from celestial bodies, questions around ownership and regulation loom large. The concept of mining in space raises complex legal and ethical issues, as no single nation or entity can claim exclusive ownership over the moon, asteroids, or any other celestial body. This principle stems from the Outer Space Treaty of 1967, a landmark agreement signed by over 100 countries, including major spacefaring nations. The treaty established that outer space, including the moon and other celestial bodies, is the "province of all humankind" and is to be used for peaceful purposes. Most importantly, it states that no country can claim sovereignty over outer space or any celestial body, effectively making them common resources for humanity.

While the Outer Space Treaty provides a broad framework, it leaves certain areas open to interpretation, particularly regarding resource extraction. The treaty does not explicitly prohibit mining or the use of resources obtained from space; it simply forbids any claims of ownership over the celestial bodies themselves. This ambiguity has created a legal gray area. If a company or country cannot claim ownership over an asteroid, then can it own the materials extracted from it? The answer to this question remains debated, as the treaty does not clarify whether entities can legally possess and profit from space resources.

Recognizing this gap, the United States took a bold step in 2015 with the passage of the U.S. Commercial Space Launch Competitiveness Act, commonly known as the Space Act of 2015. This law allows American companies to own and sell the resources they extract from space, effectively granting U.S. entities the right to claim ownership over mined materials without asserting ownership of the celestial body itself. The act sparked significant international debate, as some viewed it as an attempt to circumvent the spirit of the Outer

Space Treaty by allowing private companies to profit from what is ostensibly a global commons. Supporters of the act argue that it provides the legal certainty needed for companies to invest in space resource ventures, which could drive innovation and benefit humanity.

The Space Act of 2015 is not without limitations. It only applies to American companies and does not provide international recognition of ownership rights over mined resources. Additionally, the law raises concerns about monopolization and fair access, as other countries may follow suit with their own legislation, potentially leading to a fragmented legal landscape. Critics worry that without an international framework, a space race for resources could lead to conflicts or monopolies, where a few powerful nations or corporations control access to essential space resources.

In response to these challenges, discussions have begun around the need for a comprehensive international framework for space mining, similar to agreements on international waters. The Moon Agreement of 1979 attempted to address these issues by designating space resources as the "common heritage of mankind," implying that any benefits should be shared globally. However, the Moon Agreement has been largely ineffective, as it was not signed by major spacefaring countries, including the United States, Russia, and China. This lack of global consensus has left a void in space governance, one that becomes increasingly pressing as technological advancements bring asteroid mining closer to reality.

As the prospect of space mining grows, the international community faces the task of developing new agreements that balance national interests with the principles of shared access and sustainability. Without a clear legal structure, the future of space resources could be uncertain, leading to potential conflicts or unsustainable exploitation. The evolution of international space law will play a critical role in shaping how humanity approaches asteroid mining, ensuring that this new frontier remains open and beneficial to all.

The ethical landscape of space resource ownership is complex and uncharted, raising questions about who should benefit from the vast wealth hidden within asteroids and other celestial bodies. If asteroid mining becomes viable, it could fundamentally reshape global wealth, but the distribution of these benefits is far from straightforward. Many argue that, given space's designation as the "province of all humankind" under international treaties, resources obtained from space should be used to benefit humanity as a whole. However, the practical reality may be that only the countries and corporations with the necessary technology and financial backing will have access to these resources, potentially creating a monopoly-like structure where a few powerful entities control much of the wealth from space.

This potential for monopolization raises significant ethical concerns. If only a handful of private companies or wealthy nations gain access to space resources, they may wield disproportionate influence over essential materials that could shape industries, economies, and even the balance of power on Earth. For example, metals like platinum, cobalt, and rare earth elements, which are crucial for advanced technologies, could end up in the hands of a few corporate giants, consolidating economic and technological control. This concentration of resources might lead to global inequality, with spacefaring nations growing wealthier while others remain dependent or excluded from this new source of wealth. The ethical question then becomes whether it is just for these pioneering entities to control resources that many argue should belong to all humankind.

The debate over monopolization also extends to the environmental ethics of space mining. While mining in space could reduce the strain on Earth's resources, there is a risk that corporations might prioritize profit over sustainable practices. Without robust international oversight, asteroid mining could be pursued in ways that exhaust resources or create space debris, leading to a host of environmental challenges. This scenario raises concerns about whether corporations or nations can be trusted to manage these resources responsibly or if they will exploit them without regard for broader consequences, potentially repeating the mistakes of terrestrial resource extraction on a cosmic scale.

At the heart of these ethical dilemmas is the question of who owns space resources and who gets to decide how they are used. Currently, the global consensus on space resource ownership is fragmented. While the Outer Space Treaty provides a foundational framework by declaring space a global commons, it does not address how resources should be distributed or governed. The United States Space Act of 2015 and similar emerging legislation from countries like Luxembourg have attempted to address this by permitting companies to claim ownership of mined resources. Yet, these unilateral moves have sparked conflict, as they challenge the principles of shared access and fair use outlined in international treaties.

Navigating this landscape requires a delicate balance between fostering innovation and ensuring fair access. Nations that have not yet invested in space exploration may see the actions of spacefaring countries as a form of resource imperialism, where wealthier states extend their economic dominance into space. On the other hand, proponents of private ownership argue that allowing companies to profit from space mining is essential to drive investment and innovation in this high-risk industry. Without a clear legal framework, tensions could rise as more countries and companies seek a stake in space resources.

These conflicts underscore the need for an international regulatory framework that clarifies ownership rights, ensures equitable access, and promotes sustainable practices. Proposals for a global consortium or an intergovernmental body to oversee space mining have emerged, suggesting that resources obtained from space could be managed collectively, with profits or materials shared for the common good. Such an approach could help address ethical concerns by preventing monopolies and ensuring that all nations, not just the wealthiest or most technologically advanced, have a stake in humanity's expansion into space.

Ultimately, the way we approach space resources will reflect our collective values and priorities as a global society. Will we allow space to become another arena for monopolization and inequality, or will we take steps to ensure that the benefits of space mining are shared more equitably? These ethical and regulatory choices will define humanity's relationship with space, shaping whether asteroid mining becomes a source of collective progress or a tool for reinforcing existing disparities.

Chapter 4: Technical and Logistical Challenges

Building a mining rig for space introduces a range of engineering challenges that push the boundaries of existing technology. Unlike Earth, where gravity provides a natural anchor for equipment, space's near-zero gravity environment demands innovative solutions for even basic functions like drilling and material collection. The design of space mining rigs must account for the vacuum environment, which affects not only the equipment's functionality but also its cost and complexity.

One of the most significant challenges in rig design is adapting to zero-gravity conditions, where traditional drilling techniques fall short. In the absence of gravity, applying force on an asteroid could send the rig drifting backward or scatter particles into space, making precise material collection nearly impossible. Engineers are experimenting with anchoring mechanisms like harpoon devices that could secure a rig in place, allowing it to exert force without dislodging. Additionally, robotic arms and automated scoops designed for accurate handling of loose materials are essential, as many asteroid surfaces are irregular and brittle, requiring meticulous extraction methods.

Powering these rigs in space poses further challenges, as traditional fuel sources are impractical. Space mining equipment will likely rely on solar energy, fuel cells, or nuclear reactors to ensure continuous operation. Solar panels, a viable option, must be large enough to capture ample energy, which adds to the bulk of the rig. Each component must also be lightweight but durable enough to endure cosmic radiation, extreme temperature changes, and micrometeoroid impacts. The cost of building, testing, and deploying such specialized and resilient machinery adds a substantial financial layer to the already high expenses of space mining.

Extracting materials is only one part of the puzzle; transporting them back to Earth presents a separate set of logistical issues. Space mining transportation involves extensive fuel requirements, limited cargo capacity, and vast distances from Earth to asteroid-rich areas. Current spacecraft, such as SpaceX's Starship, have impressive cargo capacity but are not yet economically feasible for routine, high-frequency transport. For instance, valuable asteroids like 16 Psyche, located in the asteroid belt, are far from Earth, making each round trip fuel-intensive and costly.

Cargo capacity is also a critical factor. Starship's payload capacity, approximately 100 metric tons, would require thousands of trips to transport significant material quantities, which complicates large-scale operations. Each mission requires careful planning to balance fuel efficiency, trajectory corrections, and return logistics. Given the vast distances, some missions might take months or years, making the logistics of transporting materials to Earth one of the main obstacles in commercial asteroid mining.

To address these transport costs, experts are exploring ways to reduce the weight of materials that must be shipped back. One solution is processing and refining materials directly on the asteroid, minimizing the cargo size by sending back only high-value, refined metals. However, this requires additional refining equipment that must function reliably in space's harsh environment, adding yet another layer of complexity. Another idea is establishing a processing hub or storage station in low Earth orbit or on the moon, where materials could be held and then transported to Earth in smaller quantities as needed. This approach would optimize fuel use and reduce the frequency of long-haul missions from deep space.

The financial and technical challenges of developing and operating space mining rigs and managing resource transport highlight the significant hurdles in making asteroid mining economically viable.

Although technological advancements are steadily bringing this vision closer to reality, achieving it will demand pioneering breakthroughs in engineering, energy efficiency, and orbital infrastructure. Should these barriers be overcome, the wealth of resources within asteroids could ultimately provide a sustainable source for Earth's needs, laying the groundwork for a self-sustaining economy beyond our planet.

Current spacecraft, such as SpaceX's Starship, represent impressive leaps in technology but also highlight the limitations we face in making asteroid mining a practical endeavor. Starship, with its notable payload capacity of around 100 metric tons, brings us closer to the cargo needs of deep-space mining missions. Its design, with reusable stages and powerful engines, is a substantial improvement over earlier spacecraft, offering the potential for more cost-effective and frequent missions to near-Earth asteroids. However, even with these advancements, Starship—and similar existing spacecraft—are constrained by factors that limit their suitability for large-scale mining.

One key limitation is distance. Missions to asteroids located beyond Earth's immediate vicinity, such as those in the asteroid belt, require immense fuel reserves, advanced life-support systems for any crewed missions, and high durability to endure the prolonged journey. Each mission's duration and the amount of fuel needed grow considerably the farther out these mining ventures go. While Starship is optimized for journeys to the Moon and Mars, missions to the asteroid belt are considerably longer, introducing additional logistical and cost challenges. Moreover, Starship's cargo capacity, though impressive, remains small relative to the scale of resources that would make asteroid mining profitable on a global level.

To overcome these limitations, experts are looking at a range of theoretical technologies and innovative solutions to make space mining more feasible. One promising concept is in-orbit assembly, where spacecraft are launched in modular pieces and assembled in space. In-orbit assembly allows for larger, more specialized mining vehicles that are impractical to launch from Earth in a single piece. Such modular construction would allow the addition of specialized equipment for asteroid mining, including tools for anchoring, refining, and material collection. Once constructed in orbit, these mining rigs could then be sent on extended missions to asteroid-rich regions, returning only once the resources are secured and ready for transport.

Resource processing in space is another critical area of research, aimed at addressing the challenges of transporting raw materials back to Earth. By refining ores directly on the asteroid or in nearby orbit, mining operations could significantly reduce the weight and volume of materials requiring transport. This approach would involve miniaturized smelters or separation units capable of isolating high-value metals from asteroid regolith, leaving less valuable material behind. Although this technology is still in the conceptual phase, the potential benefits are significant. Processing resources in space would not only save on fuel costs but also open up the possibility of creating a space-based manufacturing economy, where raw materials are processed into components directly in orbit.

Potential vehicle advancements are also on the horizon. Concepts like nuclear propulsion, which offers higher efficiency for long-duration missions, could make deep-space mining more viable. Nuclear-powered spacecraft could maintain continuous acceleration and deceleration over extended journeys, significantly reducing the time needed for round trips to distant asteroids. Another concept under exploration is the use of electric propulsion, which, although slower, provides highly efficient fuel consumption, making it suitable for cargo transport on missions where speed is less critical. Solar sails, which use sunlight to generate propulsion, could also provide a low-energy solution for certain phases of asteroid mining, particularly when moving between orbits in the asteroid belt.

Other speculative technologies, such as asteroid-capturing mechanisms, are being considered to simplify resource transport. By moving smaller asteroids or parts of larger ones into more accessible orbits around the Moon or in low Earth orbit, mining operations could establish a stable processing zone, making it easier to break down materials and send refined products to Earth. Though capturing asteroids and placing them into controlled orbits is still largely hypothetical, advances in autonomous robotics and orbital mechanics could eventually make this feasible.

Ultimately, while spacecraft like Starship represent an essential first step, realizing large-scale asteroid mining will require a combination of advanced technologies—many of which are in the theoretical or experimental stages. In-orbit assembly, resource processing in space, and innovations in propulsion and cargo management could address the limitations of current spacecraft, making the dream of asteroid mining more than a distant possibility. These emerging technologies hint at a future where space mining is not only achievable but can sustain humanity's needs both on Earth and across a growing interplanetary economy.

Chapter 5: The Economics of Asteroid Mining

The valuation of asteroids and their resources is an exercise in both scientific analysis and economic forecasting. Experts estimate the worth of materials on asteroids by assessing the concentration and quantity of valuable elements like nickel, platinum, and water and then comparing these values to Earth-based market prices. The process involves examining spectral data collected from telescopes and space probes, which reveal an asteroid's composition by analyzing reflected light. For instance, metallic asteroids like 16 Psyche are thought to contain high concentrations of iron, nickel, and platinum, potentially worth billions or even trillions of dollars if mined and returned to Earth. Similarly, carbonaceous asteroids, rich in water and organic compounds, are valued for their potential to support space exploration by providing essential resources for life support and fuel production, reducing the need to transport these materials from Earth.

To translate these findings into market values, economists consider the global demand for these resources and their current prices. Platinum and other precious metals, which are essential in electronics and industrial applications, hold particularly high value, as their terrestrial sources are limited. For water, the value is more situational; while it may not command high prices on Earth, it is invaluable in space, where every kilogram launched incurs a substantial cost. The valuation thus considers both direct economic value and strategic significance, especially when resources could support extended space missions or contribute to constructing a sustainable infrastructure in space.

Despite the promise of high-value returns, the investment requirements for asteroid mining are daunting. Establishing a space mining operation demands a significant upfront investment in spacecraft development, mining technology, transportation systems, and potentially even orbital infrastructure like processing stations. These costs are estimated to reach into the billions, if not tens of billions, depending on the mission's scope and distance. Developing and deploying mining equipment in space, especially technology adapted for zero gravity and the vacuum of space, introduces considerable financial barriers, with substantial research and development required to ensure reliability and efficiency.

The financial risk of asteroid mining is considerable, given the high costs and untested nature of the industry. Unlike terrestrial mining, space mining involves extended timelines, complex logistics, and unpredictable conditions that could impact a mission's success. For example, unforeseen difficulties in anchoring equipment to an asteroid or efficiently extracting resources could jeopardize a mission, leading to potentially catastrophic financial losses. There's also the risk of technological failure, as space mining technology is in its infancy, with few precedents to guide design and deployment. If equipment malfunctions during a mission, the costs of repair or mission cancellation could significantly impact profitability.

Market volatility presents another risk. If space mining succeeds in bringing substantial quantities of metals like platinum to Earth, their market value may decrease due to increased supply. This effect, often referred to as "resource devaluation," could reduce the financial returns of space mining operations. For instance, a sudden influx of nickel or cobalt might lower prices, impacting profitability despite high initial investments. Asteroid mining companies must thus weigh these factors carefully, as the potential economic impact of their activities could fluctuate based on how much material they introduce into global markets and the demand for these materials at the time.

Investors interested in asteroid mining are balancing these financial risks against the potential for unprecedented returns. For those with a high-risk tolerance, the opportunity to be at the forefront of a new resource industry—especially one that could supply essential materials as Earth's reserves dwindle—holds considerable appeal. The space mining industry also attracts visionary investors who see long-term potential in establishing infrastructure in space, not only for resource extraction but also for supporting space colonization and exploration. If successful, asteroid mining could pave the way for industries in space, such as off-world manufacturing and construction, that further capitalize on the abundant resources beyond Earth.

Ultimately, the future of asteroid mining hinges on mitigating these risks through technological innovation, market foresight, and strategic partnerships. Governments may play a crucial role, either by subsidizing early-stage research or by enacting supportive policies that encourage private investment and reduce financial exposure. By addressing these investment and risk factors, the asteroid mining industry could transition from speculative endeavor to a viable commercial enterprise, fundamentally transforming how humanity sources critical materials and views the economic potential of space.

The introduction of space-sourced metals into Earth's markets has the potential to reshape economic landscapes, resource availability, and pricing structures. If asteroid mining succeeds in supplying significant quantities of materials like nickel, platinum, or rare earth elements, the global supply of these resources could increase substantially, triggering a cascade of economic effects. On one hand, the added supply could alleviate current scarcities, reduce extraction pressures on Earth, and stabilize prices for materials critical to technology and manufacturing. On the other hand, a large influx of these metals could disrupt existing industries, influence global markets, and create challenges for traditional mining economies.

One immediate impact would likely be a reduction in the scarcity of certain metals. Elements such as platinum, nickel, and cobalt are in high demand for applications in electronics, renewable energy, and aerospace, yet their availability on Earth is limited. By sourcing these materials from asteroids, where they exist in abundant and concentrated deposits, space mining could alleviate pressure on terrestrial mining operations and mitigate environmental damage caused by extracting these resources from the Earth's crust. A more stable and abundant supply of these metals could also support the growth of industries like electric vehicles and green technology, where raw material constraints currently limit production capacity and scalability.

However, an increased supply of valuable metals could have complex economic repercussions. In economic terms, when the supply of a resource increases rapidly, its market price generally decreases. For example, if a substantial quantity of platinum or cobalt were to flood the market, prices for these metals could fall. While lower prices might be beneficial for manufacturers and consumers, they could impact profitability for companies that rely on high market values, particularly terrestrial mining firms. Such a shift could lead to declining revenues in traditional mining sectors, especially in countries where mineral exports are a cornerstone of the economy, potentially prompting job losses, mine closures, and economic restructuring.

This influx of space-sourced materials could also influence global trade dynamics. Countries that are currently resource-poor may benefit from more affordable access to essential metals, potentially reducing dependence on major mineral-exporting nations. In the long term, space mining might level the playing field for countries that lack rich mineral reserves, giving them greater control over supply chains for critical resources. Conversely, nations with established mining sectors, such as Australia,

South Africa, and the Democratic Republic of Congo, may experience economic shifts if demand for terrestrial-sourced metals diminishes. This shift could spur these countries to adapt, perhaps by pivoting to new industries or investing in space mining infrastructure to remain competitive.

The impact on resource scarcity would likely be positive. By opening up a new source for metals and minerals, asteroid mining could extend the lifespan of Earth's resources, making sustainable development more achievable. The newfound abundance of critical metals could reduce the need for environmentally damaging practices, such as deep-sea mining or deforestation, which are sometimes used to extract rare minerals. For industries, this increased supply could enable more predictable production costs and support long-term planning without the looming concern of resource depletion.

However, the economic effects would be nuanced and may lead to unpredictable outcomes. If space-sourced materials drastically undercut the price of terrestrial equivalents, traditional mining companies might struggle to compete, potentially triggering consolidations or partnerships with space mining enterprises. In the long run, the arrival of space resources could prompt a shift from Earth-based extraction to space-based supply chains, transforming global resource distribution and reducing dependency on ecologically sensitive areas for raw materials. Such a transition could be slow and require significant investments in new infrastructure, but it ultimately offers the potential for an economy less reliant on Earth's finite resources.

In summary, while space-sourced metals could enhance resource security and lower costs for high-demand materials, they would also introduce new economic dynamics, influencing everything from global trade patterns to environmental impacts and industry competitiveness. The transformative effect of asteroid mining on Earth's economy highlights both the opportunities and the challenges of integrating space resources into our existing global systems. The way these changes unfold will depend on how quickly space mining technology advances, the strategies employed by industry leaders, and the policies enacted by governments to manage this unprecedented shift in resource availability.

Chapter 6: Practical Applications of Space Resources

Water is one of the most essential resources for any space mission, far surpassing its value on Earth due to its versatility and scarcity in space. In space, water is vital for sustaining life, rehydrating food, providing radiation protection, and even serving as fuel when split into hydrogen and oxygen. Astronauts rely on a continuous supply of water for drinking and hygiene, but transporting water from Earth to space is incredibly costly due to its weight, with estimates placing the cost of delivering a single liter of water to orbit at tens of thousands of dollars. Asteroid mining could provide a sustainable solution, as many carbonaceous asteroids are rich in water ice. By extracting water directly from asteroids, future space missions could establish self-sustaining water supplies, significantly reducing dependence on Earth-based resources and making long-term exploration and colonization more feasible.

Beyond its life-sustaining properties, water plays a crucial role in shielding astronauts from cosmic radiation. In deep space, radiation levels are much higher than on Earth, posing significant risks to human health on long missions. Water, with its high hydrogen content, is an effective radiation shield, absorbing harmful particles and reducing radiation exposure. Future spacecraft and space habitats could incorporate water-based shielding systems, either through water tanks or protective walls, to enhance crew safety on missions to the Moon, Mars, and beyond. This application not only maximizes the utility of water in space but also ensures the safety and well-being of crew members on extended journeys.

Water's potential as a fuel source is another game-changer. Through electrolysis, water can be split into hydrogen and oxygen, which are key components for rocket fuel. This capability opens up the possibility of creating in-space refueling stations, where water mined from asteroids or other celestial bodies is processed into fuel for interplanetary missions. Such refueling stations could allow spacecraft to travel further and return more easily, unlocking the potential for complex missions that explore deep-space regions without the need to launch with heavy fuel reserves. This approach not only reduces launch costs but also marks a step toward establishing a fully self-sufficient infrastructure in space.

The potential of asteroid resources extends beyond water to include metals, which could be used to construct infrastructure in space. Asteroids are rich in metals such as iron, nickel, and cobalt, which are crucial for building spacecraft, habitats, and other structures needed for sustained presence beyond Earth. As missions expand to explore the Moon, Mars, and possibly other parts of the solar system, transporting building materials from Earth becomes less practical. By sourcing metals directly from asteroids, it becomes feasible to build large structures in space, where they are needed, rather than incurring the high costs of launching them from Earth. This process, often referred to as in-situ resource utilization, would reduce the reliance on Earth-based resources and provide the raw materials necessary to create long-lasting, adaptable infrastructure in space.

Asteroid-sourced metals could be essential for constructing space habitats, modular outposts, and even facilities on the lunar and Martian surfaces. The construction of habitats on the Moon, for instance, would benefit immensely from locally sourced materials, as the Moon's low gravity makes it more efficient to use space-mined metals rather than terrestrial imports. Similarly, Mars colonization efforts could use asteroid resources to establish bases that provide long-term shelter and support for human settlers. These structures would not only offer protection from harsh space environments but also foster independence from Earth's supply chains, a critical factor in the success of any off-world colony.

Asteroid mining for infrastructure metals also opens the door to large-scale projects that would otherwise be constrained by cost or engineering limitations. Concepts such as space-based solar power stations, which would require massive metal frameworks, become more feasible if the raw materials can be sourced and assembled in orbit. Additionally, manufacturing and assembling components in space would allow for structures that could not survive the stresses of Earth's gravity and atmospheric re-entry, enabling the construction of larger, more complex facilities than previously possible. This space-based infrastructure could form the backbone of an interplanetary transportation network, complete with stations, repair facilities, and habitats for both humans and robotic systems.

In essence, water and metals from asteroids are pivotal resources that could transform the scope and ambition of human space exploration. Water supports life, shields against radiation, and fuels spacecraft, while metals lay the groundwork for robust, sustainable infrastructure in space. Together, they represent the foundation of a self-sustaining space economy, providing humanity with the means to explore, settle, and build beyond our home planet. By utilizing the resources already present in space, future missions can reduce costs, extend their reach, and advance toward a future where humanity is no longer bound to Earth.

Space manufacturing is a transformative opportunity that could redefine the way humanity approaches construction, resource utilization, and mission logistics in space. With abundant materials sourced from asteroids, it becomes increasingly feasible to produce essential components directly in space rather than launching them from Earth. The implications of off-world manufacturing are vast: from constructing spacecraft and habitats to producing fuel and specialized parts, the ability to build in space could significantly reduce costs, increase efficiency, and accelerate humanity's expansion beyond Earth.

The prospect of space manufacturing begins with asteroid mining, where resources like metals and water can be harvested directly from celestial bodies. Metals such as iron, nickel, and cobalt, which are found abundantly in metallic and silicaceous asteroids, could serve as the foundational materials for constructing various components and structures in orbit. Instead of relying on Earth's limited resources and bearing the high cost of transporting heavy materials, space-based manufacturing facilities could use these raw materials to produce everything from support beams and structural frameworks to the delicate circuitry required for advanced equipment. By establishing processing plants and manufacturing units in orbit or on the lunar surface, space manufacturing could facilitate the creation of large, durable, and cost-effective structures without the constraints of gravity and launch capacity limitations.

Water, also obtainable from certain types of asteroids, holds immense value for off-world production. Through electrolysis, water can be converted into hydrogen and oxygen, which can then be used as fuel for propulsion systems. In the context of space manufacturing, this capability means that refueling stations could be established in orbit, enabling spacecraft to make extended journeys or return trips without carrying all the necessary fuel from Earth. In addition to providing fuel, water is also essential for cooling systems in manufacturing processes and for supporting life in space habitats, thereby playing a multi-faceted role in enabling manufacturing operations.

One of the most promising applications of space manufacturing is the in-situ production of spacecraft and modular components. Constructing spacecraft in space eliminates the need to design them to withstand Earth's launch stresses, allowing for the development of structures that are optimized for the space environment rather than for the rigors of atmospheric re-entry. In-orbit manufacturing could thus lead to the creation of larger, more sophisticated spacecraft that would be impractical to launch from Earth. This capability would not only support more complex missions but also allow for quick repairs and upgrades, reducing the downtime and cost associated with transporting replacement parts from Earth.

Space manufacturing also opens doors for building habitats and support facilities for long-term exploration. With access to locally sourced metals, it becomes feasible to create habitats on the Moon, Mars, or even in deep space. These habitats could be constructed with thick walls for radiation shielding, water reserves for life support, and metal frameworks for structural stability—all produced and assembled in situ. Additionally, constructing habitats directly in space or on extraterrestrial surfaces allows for design flexibility and scalability, enabling habitats to be expanded or modified based on mission needs without relying on a constant stream of shipments from Earth.

The concept of "just-in-time" manufacturing in space is also gaining traction, where parts are produced on-demand rather than stockpiled. This approach would allow missions to carry only essential tools and raw materials, significantly reducing payload mass and launch costs. Advanced manufacturing techniques such as 3D printing are already being tested for this purpose. With 3D printers designed for microgravity, parts, tools, and even replacement components could be created on-site as needed, rather than transported from Earth. This flexibility is particularly advantageous for missions to distant locations like Mars, where resupply options are limited.

Space manufacturing also offers a pathway to sustainable off-world economies, with a focus on self-sufficiency and the minimization of Earth dependence. By using asteroid-derived materials, future missions could develop a robust manufacturing ecosystem that supports the production of essential goods and services beyond our planet. From building communications infrastructure and solar power arrays to producing radiation shields and agricultural equipment, off-world manufacturing would be key in supporting sustained human presence and fostering a thriving space economy.

The long-term potential of space manufacturing extends to industries like space tourism and interplanetary trade, where space-assembled vehicles and facilities could become essential. A manufacturing base in orbit could eventually produce everything from the structural components of space hotels to cargo ships designed for interplanetary routes. By developing manufacturing infrastructure in space, humanity could create an interconnected economy that spans Earth, the Moon, Mars, and beyond, with a network of resources, products, and services that enable seamless movement and trade across these realms.

In essence, space manufacturing transforms resource availability into a practical asset, allowing humanity to move beyond the limits of Earth's supply chain. By supporting the production of parts, fuel, and essential components, it lays the groundwork for self-sustaining infrastructure, resilient exploration, and long-term expansion into the cosmos. As technology advances and space manufacturing facilities are realized, the dream of building and thriving in space becomes an achievable reality, setting the stage for an era of interplanetary industry and exploration.

Chapter 7: The Environmental and Societal Impact on Earth

The prospect of shifting resource extraction from Earth to space offers a significant opportunity for environmental relief, with the potential to alleviate some of the most pressing ecological pressures facing our planet. Traditional mining and resource extraction industries are responsible for a range of environmental impacts, from deforestation and habitat destruction to water pollution and greenhouse gas emissions. By relocating the extraction of critical metals and minerals to asteroids, humanity could reduce the strain on Earth's ecosystems, preserving biodiversity, reducing pollution, and mitigating climate change effects.

One of the most immediate benefits of space-based resource extraction would be a reduction in habitat destruction. Terrestrial mining operations often require clearing large tracts of land, leading to deforestation and loss of biodiversity. Rainforests, boreal forests, and other sensitive ecosystems have been heavily impacted by mining activities, with local wildlife populations suffering due to habitat fragmentation and degradation. As asteroid mining reduces the need for Earth-based mineral extraction, vast areas of land could be preserved, protecting habitats and supporting efforts to conserve biodiversity.

Water pollution is another serious consequence of terrestrial mining, particularly in regions where valuable metals like cobalt, lithium, and gold are extracted. Mining processes frequently introduce toxic chemicals, such as mercury and cyanide, into nearby rivers and groundwater, affecting aquatic ecosystems and threatening the health of communities that rely on these water sources. If we could source metals like cobalt, nickel, and platinum from asteroids instead, the impact on freshwater ecosystems would be greatly reduced. This shift would allow water systems to recover, creating healthier environments for aquatic life and reducing risks to human health.

Beyond the direct environmental impacts of mining, the energy-intensive nature of resource extraction also contributes to global greenhouse gas emissions, particularly when fossil fuels are burned to power mining equipment and processing facilities. These emissions play a substantial role in driving climate change, affecting ecosystems around the world through rising temperatures, sea level rise, and increased frequency of extreme weather events. Moving mining operations to space would significantly reduce these emissions, as space mining could rely on solar energy rather than fossil fuels. Solar-powered mining rigs and processing facilities operating in space could help decouple resource extraction from greenhouse gas emissions, allowing industries to meet their material needs without contributing to global warming.

Moreover, as space mining technology advances, it could provide resources essential for green technologies on Earth. Metals such as lithium, cobalt, and nickel are critical for renewable energy solutions, including solar panels, wind turbines, and batteries for electric vehicles. Increased access to these resources through asteroid mining could accelerate the transition to clean energy, reducing our reliance on fossil fuels and helping mitigate the climate crisis. By enabling a sustainable supply of these metals without further damaging Earth's ecosystems, space mining could support both environmental preservation and technological advancement.

The shift to space-based resource extraction could also reduce the economic incentives for environmentally damaging practices like deep-sea mining, which threatens ocean ecosystems. With rising demand for metals, some companies have started exploring the ocean floor, a practice that risks devastating impacts on marine life and underwater ecosystems that remain poorly understood. By providing an alternative, space mining could make it economically feasible to leave these sensitive ocean regions undisturbed, contributing to marine conservation efforts and protecting one of the planet's last unexplored frontiers.

In summary, relocating resource extraction to space has the potential to relieve many of the environmental pressures associated with traditional mining. By reducing habitat destruction, curtailing water pollution, lowering greenhouse gas emissions, and preserving marine ecosystems, asteroid mining could enable humanity to meet its resource needs in a way that is far more sustainable and ecologically responsible. This transition would represent a profound shift, allowing Earth's ecosystems to recover while supporting the growth of green technologies essential for a sustainable future. In this way, space mining not only offers economic promise but also stands as a pivotal opportunity to protect and restore the planet we call home.

Asteroid mining has the potential to address some of the fundamental drivers of global inequality by providing a vast new source of critical resources, which could, in turn, reduce resource-based conflicts and elevate living standards around the world. On Earth, access to metals and minerals is often geographically limited, with certain countries holding the majority of economically viable reserves of materials like cobalt, lithium, and platinum. This concentration of resources has historically led to geopolitical tensions, economic dependency, and, in some cases, exploitation of both land and labor. By shifting to space-based resource extraction, humanity could unlock an abundance of these materials, potentially leveling the playing field and decreasing the imbalance created by resource scarcity.

One of the primary ways asteroid mining could mitigate global inequality is by reducing dependency on resource-rich regions. Countries that currently lack access to critical minerals could benefit from a more equitable distribution of space-sourced resources. With increased supply, global prices for essential metals may stabilize, making these resources more affordable for developing nations and enabling broader access to advanced technologies. Access to affordable metals is especially relevant in the context of green technology, as it could help developing countries participate in renewable energy initiatives, enhance their infrastructure, and improve public services that depend on advanced technology.

Additionally, asteroid mining could diminish the economic pressures that contribute to resource-based conflicts. Many regions rich in valuable minerals have faced political instability, conflict, and corruption tied to control over these resources. As asteroid mining reduces Earth's reliance on these materials, the economic incentives fueling these conflicts could decrease, paving the way for more peaceful and stable development in affected areas. In the long term, a reliable supply of metals and minerals from space could support global development goals, giving more countries the means to grow their economies without depleting finite terrestrial resources or engaging in unsustainable practices.

However, the concept of space mining also brings with it questions about ownership, access, and fair distribution. While asteroid mining has the potential to benefit humanity as a whole, there is a risk that its advantages could become concentrated among wealthy nations and corporations, thereby perpetuating inequalities rather than reducing them. Without a well-defined international framework governing space resources, there is a possibility that the benefits of asteroid mining could be monopolized, favoring those with the means to access and exploit space-based resources. Ensuring that the fruits of space mining are shared equitably will require cooperation, transparency, and agreements that prioritize the common good over private interests.

Public perception and acceptance of asteroid mining will be critical to its development, with the media, environmental groups, and general public likely to play influential roles in shaping how society views this new industry. The media, as one of the primary conveyors of information, has the power to frame asteroid mining as either a groundbreaking step toward sustainable progress or as a potential ecological and ethical hazard. Positive media coverage, focusing on the environmental benefits, economic opportunities, and technological advancements that space mining could bring, may foster widespread public support and enthusiasm for the industry. However, if coverage emphasizes the risks, costs, or potential for inequality, public skepticism could grow, potentially influencing policy and slowing industry progress.

Environmental groups are another key factor in shaping public attitudes. While asteroid mining promises a reduction in the environmental impacts of terrestrial extraction, concerns remain about the long-term ecological consequences of space mining, particularly the potential for increased space debris and resource exploitation in space. Environmental organizations, which are likely to advocate for sustainable practices and responsible regulation, may support asteroid mining if it demonstrably benefits Earth's ecosystems and reduces pollution. However, without clear commitments to environmental safeguards, these groups could voice opposition, pushing for tighter oversight and regulations to prevent potential harms associated with space operations.

Public opinion on asteroid mining will ultimately hinge on perceptions of its necessity, equity, and impact. The general public is increasingly aware of the environmental challenges posed by traditional mining and may view asteroid mining as a forward-looking solution that aligns with sustainability goals. However, as with any emerging technology, public acceptance may be tempered by concerns about monopolization, job displacement in traditional mining industries, and ethical questions surrounding humanity's expansion into space. Public trust in the industry could be fostered through transparency, inclusive international agreements, and a clear commitment to sharing the benefits of space resources equitably.

In conclusion, asteroid mining holds the promise of reducing global inequalities by offering a more abundant and accessible supply of critical resources, potentially curbing conflicts and supporting sustainable development worldwide. However, the way this industry is regulated, perceived, and executed will determine whether its benefits are truly shared or concentrated among a select few. Balancing technological innovation with ethical and environmental considerations will be essential to gaining public acceptance and ensuring that asteroid mining contributes positively to both global prosperity and planetary stewardship.

Chapter 8: Case Studies and Experiments in Space Mining

Asteroid exploration has advanced significantly over the past two decades, with successful missions paving the way for potential resource extraction and a deeper understanding of these celestial bodies. Key missions, such as Japan's Hayabusa programs and NASA's OSIRIS-REx mission, have achieved remarkable breakthroughs, returning asteroid samples to Earth and providing valuable insights into the composition, structure, and potential resources of near-Earth asteroids. These pioneering efforts underscore the feasibility of reaching, studying, and even extracting materials from asteroids—critical steps toward the realization of space mining.

The Japanese Hayabusa missions marked a significant leap in asteroid exploration. The first Hayabusa mission, launched by the Japan Aerospace Exploration Agency (JAXA) in 2003, was designed to rendezvous with the asteroid Itokawa, a near-Earth object. Hayabusa successfully reached Itokawa in 2005 and made history as the first mission to land on an asteroid, collect samples, and return them to Earth. However, the mission was not without challenges; technical issues with the sampling mechanism and propulsion system posed considerable obstacles. Despite these setbacks, Hayabusa ultimately returned a small sample of asteroid material in 2010, providing the first direct look at an asteroid's surface composition and inspiring confidence in the feasibility of future asteroid missions.

Building on the success of Hayabusa, JAXA launched Hayabusa2 in 2014, targeting the asteroid Ryugu, a carbon-rich asteroid that could offer clues about the early solar system. Hayabusa2 reached Ryugu in 2018 and carried out a series of complex operations, including deploying small rovers to gather surface data, firing a projectile to create an artificial crater, and collecting samples from both the surface and subsurface. Hayabusa2's achievements were remarkable, and the mission successfully returned to Earth in 2020 with samples from Ryugu. Analysis of these samples revealed organic compounds and hydrated minerals, highlighting the potential of asteroids as sources of water and carbon-based materials that could be valuable for future space exploration and off-Earth resource utilization.

NASA's OSIRIS-REx mission further advanced the field of asteroid research, targeting the asteroid Bennu, a near-Earth asteroid with a composition similar to carbonaceous chondrites. OSIRIS-REx launched in 2016 and arrived at Bennu in 2018, where it spent nearly two years mapping the asteroid's surface and studying its composition. In October 2020, OSIRIS-REx performed a successful sample collection, capturing material from Bennu's surface in a process known as a "touch-and-go" maneuver. The mission's sample return capsule arrived on Earth in 2023, delivering a substantial quantity of Bennu material for study. Early analysis of the samples has shown that Bennu contains carbon-rich compounds and hydrated minerals, reinforcing the potential of similar asteroids to provide water and carbon in future space missions. OSIRIS-REx also provided critical data on Bennu's orbit, rotation, and surface properties, contributing valuable knowledge that could aid in future asteroid exploration and mining efforts.

In addition to these flagship missions, there have been several other pioneering efforts in asteroid exploration. The European Space Agency (ESA) launched its Rosetta mission in 2004, initially aimed at studying a comet but providing valuable insights into space navigation and resource utilization techniques applicable to asteroid missions. Rosetta's close study of comet 67P/Churyumov-Gerasimenko included surface mapping, organic material detection, and direct sampling, laying groundwork for future missions that may need to interact with similarly challenging small-body environments.

Together, these missions have proven that it is possible to reach, study, and return samples from asteroids, despite the unique challenges posed by these small, distant, and low-gravity objects. Each mission has contributed to refining the techniques, tools, and technology needed to carry out successful asteroid operations, from precise navigation and sampling mechanisms to surface landing techniques and sample retrieval. The data gathered from these missions offers a valuable foundation for assessing the feasibility of asteroid mining, particularly for identifying resource-rich targets and understanding the logistical challenges involved.

The success of Hayabusa, Hayabusa2, OSIRIS-REx, and other exploratory missions demonstrates the potential for more ambitious missions that could lead to sustainable resource extraction from asteroids. As technological capabilities continue to advance, these pioneering efforts serve as proof-of-concept, inspiring new missions and driving forward the vision of a future where asteroid mining supports both Earth's industries and humanity's exploration of the cosmos.

The ambitious vision of asteroid mining has attracted private companies eager to turn the concept into reality, though early efforts have highlighted the considerable challenges inherent in this field. Companies like Planetary Resources and Deep Space Industries led the charge, developing plans to prospect and eventually mine valuable resources from near-Earth asteroids. While their ventures generated excitement and demonstrated the potential for a new space-based economy, these companies faced numerous obstacles related to technology, financing, and the practical realities of mining in space, underscoring the difficulties of building a viable asteroid mining industry from the ground up.

Planetary Resources, founded in 2012, was one of the most high-profile companies to pursue asteroid mining. Its mission was to identify and eventually mine asteroids rich in valuable resources, such as water and metals like platinum and nickel. Planetary Resources attracted significant investment and high-profile backers, including Google co-founders Larry Page and Eric Schmidt, fueling optimism about the industry's potential. The company developed and launched several demonstration satellites, including the Arkyd series, designed to test technologies for asteroid prospecting and data collection. However, Planetary Resources struggled with the high costs of development and the slow pace of technological advancements needed to make mining feasible. Ultimately, despite its ambitious plans, the company pivoted to Earth observation and was eventually acquired by a blockchain company in 2018, highlighting the challenge of sustaining a business in an emerging field that requires extensive, long-term investment.

Deep Space Industries (DSI), another pioneering company founded in 2013, focused on developing technologies for space resource utilization. DSI envisioned a multi-stage approach to asteroid mining, starting with small spacecraft to prospect and analyze potential targets before scaling up to more robust mining operations. The company planned to leverage water and metals from asteroids to support space-based infrastructure, such as fuel depots and manufacturing facilities. DSI successfully launched several demonstration missions to test technologies related to asteroid prospecting and in-space propulsion. Despite its progress, DSI faced similar challenges to those encountered by Planetary Resources, including high costs, limited revenue streams, and the long timelines required to achieve profitability. DSI was ultimately acquired by Bradford Space in 2019, which redirected its focus toward in-space propulsion systems rather than asteroid mining, illustrating the steep challenges for early players in the industry.

These early ventures by private companies provided valuable lessons about the practical and financial hurdles in asteroid mining. While Planetary Resources and Deep Space Industries helped raise awareness and advance the conversation around space resource utilization, the technical challenges, regulatory uncertainties, and significant capital requirements remain formidable barriers. The experiences of these companies have made it clear that asteroid mining will likely require advancements in space technology, substantial investment, and robust partnerships with public sector entities to succeed.

Despite these early setbacks, asteroid mining continues to attract interest, and new missions and proposals are underway, with public agencies and private enterprises collaborating to explore the field further. NASA's Psyche mission, scheduled for launch in 2022, aims to explore the metallic asteroid 16 Psyche, located in the asteroid belt between Mars and Jupiter. Psyche is believed to be the exposed core of a protoplanet, offering a unique opportunity to study a metal-rich asteroid and gain insights into planetary formation. Although the mission is primarily scientific, the data collected could be invaluable for understanding the composition and mining potential of metal-rich asteroids, advancing the knowledge needed for future resource extraction missions.

The European Space Agency (ESA) is also contributing to asteroid research with its Hera mission, planned as part of the AIDA (Asteroid Impact & Deflection Assessment) collaboration with NASA. Hera will study the effects of NASA's DART mission, which aims to impact the moonlet of the binary asteroid Didymos, providing valuable data on asteroid dynamics and composition. While not directly focused on mining, Hera's observations could inform the engineering and operational strategies needed to interact safely and effectively with small bodies in space.

Private sector initiatives have also emerged, with new companies exploring business models that might circumvent some of the challenges faced by early pioneers. For instance, TransAstra, a U.S.-based company, has proposed an approach known as "optical mining," which uses concentrated sunlight to extract water and other volatile compounds from asteroids. This process could be used to create fuel depots in space, enabling refueling stations that support deep-space exploration. Though still in the conceptual phase, such innovations represent a shift in thinking—focusing on incremental advancements and specific goals like water extraction rather than fully developed mining operations, which could be more viable in the near term.

Speculative projects are also on the horizon, with some companies proposing long-term plans to capture and redirect small asteroids into orbits closer to Earth or the Moon for easier access. This concept would enable closer observation and, potentially, controlled mining operations in a more accessible environment. Such approaches are years, if not decades, from realization, but they reflect the industry's willingness to think creatively about overcoming the logistical and technical challenges of asteroid mining.

While these missions and proposals illustrate different pathways toward space resource utilization, the journey toward economically viable asteroid mining is likely to be gradual. As public and private entities continue to test technologies, develop partnerships, and gather data from pioneering missions, each step will contribute to building the foundation for a future where asteroid mining supports human expansion into space. These efforts underscore that asteroid mining remains an ambitious yet achievable goal, one that will require patience, investment, and collaboration to transform from a speculative vision into a practical industry.

Chapter 9: Future Perspectives: From Speculation to Reality

The viability of asteroid mining hinges on a series of technological advancements that will enable efficient resource extraction, processing, and transport in space. While significant progress has been made in space exploration, mining asteroids on a commercial scale requires specialized technology to overcome unique challenges such as low gravity, distance from Earth, and limited fuel resources. If these innovations continue to advance, asteroid mining could transition from theory to practice within the coming decades, potentially opening a new frontier of sustainable resource acquisition and space infrastructure.

One of the primary technological advancements required for asteroid mining is in spacecraft propulsion. Current chemical propulsion systems are costly and fuel-intensive, limiting the feasibility of deep-space missions where mining opportunities are most promising. Advanced propulsion technologies, such as nuclear thermal propulsion or solar electric propulsion, could significantly extend mission durations, reduce fuel requirements, and enable spacecraft to reach and return from distant asteroid targets efficiently. Nuclear thermal propulsion, for instance, offers much higher thrust and efficiency compared to chemical rockets, making it ideal for long-duration missions. Solar electric propulsion, although slower, could be suitable for cargo transport between Earth and asteroid-rich regions, as it is highly efficient and can operate over extended periods using solar energy.

Another essential innovation lies in robotics and autonomous systems. Mining in space will require highly specialized robotic equipment capable of extracting materials without human intervention, as asteroid mining missions will often be too remote for real-time human control. Autonomous systems for anchoring, drilling, and collecting materials will need to operate reliably in low-gravity environments, where traditional mining techniques fail. Advances in artificial intelligence and machine learning will also play a key role, enabling robotic systems to adapt to the irregular terrain and dynamic conditions of asteroid surfaces. Prototypes of autonomous mining robots and sample collection devices are already under development, with agencies like NASA testing robots that could one day be deployed on asteroids.

Resource processing and in-situ utilization technologies are also critical to the feasibility of asteroid mining. Rather than transporting raw materials directly back to Earth, processing the materials on-site could significantly reduce transport costs by separating valuable resources from waste. Techniques such as "optical mining," which uses focused sunlight to extract water and other volatiles from asteroid regolith, have shown promise for in-situ resource processing. In addition, the development of in-orbit refineries and miniaturized smelting facilities capable of operating in low-gravity environments could make it possible to process metals, extract fuel, and prepare usable materials before they are transported back to Earth or used in space-based manufacturing.

Another key development is the establishment of infrastructure in space, such as refueling stations, processing facilities, and storage depots, which would support long-term asteroid mining operations. The construction of a lunar or orbital processing hub, for instance, would allow mined materials to be stored and refined in space, reducing the frequency of costly trips to Earth and enabling a sustainable supply chain within the space environment. These hubs could serve as the foundation for a new kind of industrial network in space, where raw materials are gathered, processed, and used for construction or manufacturing on-site, further minimizing transport costs.

Speculating on the timeline for large-scale asteroid mining involves estimating both technological progress and economic viability. In the next 10 to

20 years, advancements in autonomous mining technology, propulsion, and resource processing could enable experimental mining missions to begin. During this period, governments and private enterprises may conduct small-scale operations to test equipment, refine mining techniques, and validate the economic potential of extracting resources from asteroids. NASA's upcoming Psyche mission and other exploratory projects are expected to deliver critical data on asteroid composition and structure, informing future mining endeavors. Early pilot missions may focus on water extraction and simple processing tasks to supply fuel and materials for spacecraft, thus providing a foundation for more ambitious operations.

Looking further ahead, large-scale asteroid mining could realistically begin in the 2040s or 2050s, provided that technological milestones are achieved and supportive economic and legal frameworks are established. By then, advances in propulsion, robotics, and processing facilities, combined with the construction of orbital infrastructure, could make sustained mining operations feasible. Companies may initially target nearby asteroids that are rich in water and metals, using mined resources to support a growing space economy, including activities like satellite maintenance, space station resupply, and in-orbit construction.

The potential for asteroid mining to become an integral part of human industry depends not only on technological readiness but also on the market demand for space-sourced materials, international cooperation, and regulatory support. The expansion of lunar and Martian exploration, commercial space travel, and the development of sustainable energy technologies on Earth will all influence the demand for resources that asteroid mining can supply. If these trends align, the mid-century could see the rise of a space-based economy where mining asteroids is a routine and economically viable enterprise.

Ultimately, asteroid mining's transition from speculative possibility to reality represents humanity's next frontier, a step that could redefine our relationship with space and create a sustainable pathway to explore, develop, and live beyond Earth. While the timeline remains uncertain and hinges on technological and regulatory developments, the innovations required to make asteroid mining feasible are within reach, and the coming decades hold the potential for profound advancements that may shape a new era of space exploration and resource sustainability.

Humanity's journey into space represents a profound shift, both philosophically and practically, as we move from an Earth-centered existence toward a future where space plays a fundamental role in sustaining life, advancing technology, and expanding human presence. The ability to harness the resources of space, particularly through asteroid mining and in-situ resource utilization, is a critical step in this evolution. As we access the metals, water, and minerals from asteroids and other celestial bodies, we open up new possibilities for establishing self-sufficient colonies on the Moon, Mars, and potentially even further into the cosmos.

Philosophically, space exploration challenges us to rethink our place in the universe and our relationship with Earth's resources. For centuries, our survival and progress have been closely tied to the planet's limited resources, which has led to cycles of consumption, scarcity, and environmental degradation. The prospect of accessing space resources offers an alternative path—one that could alleviate pressure on Earth's ecosystems, shift our thinking from resource limitation to abundance, and inspire a new era of technological and societal growth. If we can build a sustainable infrastructure in space, humanity could move beyond its dependence on Earth's finite materials, fostering a mindset that values exploration, stewardship, and responsible innovation.

This shift also prompts a reevaluation of our role as stewards not only of Earth but of the solar system. The ethical considerations surrounding space resource utilization are complex, as we must decide how to balance exploration with preservation. This new frontier calls for a framework of responsibility and equity, ensuring that the benefits of space resources are shared globally and that humanity approaches space with a commitment to protect and respect the celestial environments we encounter.

Practically, harnessing space resources has transformative implications for our capacity to explore and colonize other planets. With water, metals, and energy sources mined directly from asteroids or lunar soil, we can build the infrastructure needed for long-term survival in space without the prohibitive cost of transporting all materials from Earth. Water extracted from asteroids or Mars's polar ice caps could be used for drinking, agriculture, and shielding against cosmic radiation. Electrolysis of water would provide oxygen for breathing and hydrogen for fuel, supporting self-sustaining colonies with minimal dependency on Earth for basic needs. These capabilities lay the groundwork for permanent outposts on Mars and the Moon, where humans can live, work, and eventually expand further.

The construction of space habitats, refueling stations, and industrial facilities in orbit or on the lunar surface would create a network that enables deeper space exploration. This infrastructure could serve as a launchpad for missions to Mars and beyond, allowing spacecraft to refuel, receive repairs, and undergo maintenance without needing to return to Earth. The ability to manufacture parts and equipment in space from asteroid-derived materials would reduce launch costs and make large-scale, long-distance missions economically viable. In this way, space resources provide the essential building blocks for an interplanetary civilization, where travel between celestial bodies becomes routine and sustainable.

Mars colonization, one of humanity's most ambitious goals, becomes more feasible as space mining and resource utilization technologies develop. Establishing a colony on Mars would require significant resources, from construction materials and radiation shielding to food and water supplies. By using materials sourced from Mars itself and nearby asteroids, a Mars colony could gradually reduce its dependence on Earth and evolve into a self-sustaining society. This would not only provide a backup location for humanity in the event of planetary catastrophes but also offer a platform for scientific research and exploration of the Martian surface and beyond.

Beyond Mars, harnessing space resources opens up the possibility of exploring the outer solar system, where moons like Europa and Enceladus hold intriguing scientific interest and could serve as waypoints for deeper space missions. The establishment of a sustainable presence on these distant worlds would likely require both advanced technology and a space-based resource economy that supports the high demands of life far from Earth. As humanity develops the capacity to live off the land in space, each step takes us closer to becoming a multi-planetary species, spreading human presence across the solar system and, perhaps one day, reaching neighboring star systems.

Ultimately, humanity's space-bound future is not just about survival or economic gain; it is about expanding the boundaries of human potential. As we harness space resources, we lay the groundwork for a civilization that transcends the limitations of our home planet, driven by the desire to explore, understand, and thrive in the vast cosmos. This journey requires vision, collaboration, and a commitment to shared values that ensure space benefits all of humanity. By tapping into the resources of space, we embrace the possibility of a world where human ingenuity and resilience continue to propel us forward, transforming both ourselves and our place in the universe.

Chapter 10: Challenges and Potential Risks Ahead

The prospect of asteroid mining is enticing, promising untapped wealth and abundant resources, yet it remains fraught with significant economic risks that can lead to investor skepticism. The high upfront costs, extended timelines, and unpredictable returns make asteroid mining a high-risk venture, even for those with a visionary outlook. For investors, the prospect of committing large sums of capital to a field that lacks a proven business model can be daunting, especially given the numerous financial, technical, and regulatory uncertainties.

One of the primary economic risks lies in the substantial initial investment required. Developing and launching the technology to reach, mine, and transport resources from asteroids is a costly endeavor, with estimates suggesting that early missions could require billions of dollars in investment. Companies must fund spacecraft development, advanced robotics, propulsion systems, and in-space processing infrastructure, all of which are still in early stages of development. Moreover, each component must be engineered to withstand the harsh conditions of space, from extreme temperatures to radiation, adding further to the cost. Unlike other high-risk investments, where returns might be projected within a few years, asteroid mining requires extended timelines, with returns potentially taking decades to materialize.

The timeline itself presents a serious challenge for investors. Space missions are inherently time-intensive, often taking years just to reach target asteroids, let alone complete mining operations and return materials to Earth. The lengthy duration of these missions introduces numerous risks, from the possibility of technological failures to unforeseen delays caused by environmental or technical issues. These prolonged timelines make it difficult for investors to see returns on their capital in the near future, limiting the appeal for those seeking quicker or more predictable gains.

Another significant risk is the uncertainty surrounding the value of resources that would be mined from asteroids. While estimates of metal concentrations and potential yields from asteroids are promising, they remain speculative. Spectral analysis and other remote sensing techniques provide an approximate idea of an asteroid's composition, but the true value and quantity of extractable resources can only be confirmed upon arrival. There is a risk that the target asteroids may yield less than expected or that mining processes could be more challenging than anticipated, thereby impacting the financial viability of the mission.

Moreover, market volatility adds to the uncertainty. If space mining introduces large quantities of metals like platinum, cobalt, or nickel into global markets, it could cause a reduction in their prices, impacting returns. This potential "devaluation effect" means that the very success of asteroid mining could undermine its profitability, as increased supply would likely drive down the market value of these metals. Investors must, therefore, weigh the possibility that even a successful mining mission might not yield the anticipated financial returns due to fluctuations in commodity prices.

Investor skepticism is also fueled by the lack of established regulatory frameworks. The legal and ownership rights over resources extracted from space remain ambiguous, creating an environment of uncertainty around property rights and taxation. While some legislation, such as the U.S. Space Act of 2015, allows American companies to own and profit from materials mined in space, it does not provide international recognition or cover the complexities of cross-border resource trade. Without a globally recognized legal framework, companies and investors could face regulatory challenges that add to the uncertainty surrounding potential returns.

Given these risks, it is no surprise that investor skepticism is a recurring theme in discussions about asteroid mining. Many investors view space mining as a speculative venture, with high-stakes risks that might outweigh potential gains. To overcome this skepticism, companies involved in space mining may need to develop phased business models that focus initially on lower-risk activities, such as remote sensing and prospecting services, before advancing to full-scale mining operations. Demonstrating proof of concept through smaller, incremental successes could help build investor confidence and attract the necessary funding to move forward.

In summary, the economic risks of asteroid mining stem from high investment costs, lengthy and uncertain timelines, unpredictable resource yields, market volatility, and regulatory ambiguity. These challenges make it a difficult sell for investors, who must be willing to commit capital to a highly uncertain and long-term endeavor. However, with continued advancements in technology, strategic partnerships, and incremental successes, asteroid mining may eventually become a more attractive investment, potentially paving the way for humanity's next great economic frontier.

Asteroid mining, while promising, is accompanied by significant risks of technological and operational failures that could jeopardize missions and investment. The process of reaching, mining, and returning resources from an asteroid is technologically complex, involving many systems that must function seamlessly in harsh, unpredictable space environments. Even with extensive planning, there is always a risk of mission failure due to technological breakdowns, environmental conditions, or unforeseen challenges, making the venture financially and operationally precarious.

One major risk lies in the extreme conditions of space itself, where equipment must operate reliably under intense radiation, temperature fluctuations, and microgravity. Mining rigs, robotic arms, and autonomous systems for drilling, collecting, and processing materials must withstand these conditions for extended periods without direct human intervention. A single malfunction in critical systems—whether in propulsion, anchoring, or mining mechanisms—could lead to mission failure. If, for instance, a mining rig fails to anchor itself securely to an asteroid's low-gravity surface, it might drift off course, making resource collection impossible. Likewise, if propulsion systems or fuel reserves become compromised, a spacecraft might be unable to complete its journey or return with the collected materials, leading to a total mission loss.

Operational failures are also a real threat in the complex, autonomous systems required for space mining. Robotic technologies in space must adapt to unforeseen challenges, such as irregular asteroid surfaces, which can make navigation and extraction difficult. Autonomous systems are improving, but the lack of real-time control due to communication delays with Earth makes it challenging to correct issues that arise on the spot. Additionally, unexpected events, such as collisions with micrometeoroids or debris, could damage equipment or even cause catastrophic failure, further illustrating the risks and the need for robust, resilient technology.

Beyond the technological challenges, asteroid mining introduces moral and environmental concerns that require careful consideration. One of the foremost ethical questions centers on humanity's expansion into space and the potential consequences of treating it as a new frontier for resource extraction. Some argue that we risk repeating the mistakes made on Earth—such as environmental degradation and resource depletion—by exploiting celestial bodies without fully understanding the long-term impacts. Mining operations in space may seem removed from Earth's ecosystems, but they could still create unintended consequences, including increased space debris and disruptions to the cosmic environment.

The creation of space debris is one of the most immediate environmental risks associated with asteroid mining. Mining equipment, fragments from drilling operations, and other byproducts could remain in orbit, contributing to the existing problem of space debris. This debris poses hazards not only to mining missions but also to satellites, space stations, and future missions traveling through affected regions. As the amount of debris grows, the likelihood of collisions increases, raising concerns about safety and sustainability. Without careful debris management and orbital planning, asteroid mining could exacerbate these risks, making some parts of space hazardous or even unusable.

Additionally, there are concerns about the potential alteration of the cosmic environment. While asteroids may seem lifeless, they contain materials that have been preserved since the solar system's formation, offering invaluable scientific insight. Mining these bodies could disrupt or eliminate sources of knowledge before they have been fully studied. Moreover, the long-term impacts of extracting resources from asteroids are unknown, as humanity has never attempted to modify other celestial bodies on this scale. For example, large-scale extraction could theoretically alter an asteroid's mass or trajectory, possibly affecting its gravitational interactions with other objects. Although these risks are still speculative, they underscore the importance of cautious and responsible practices.

Ethically, the expansion into asteroid mining also raises questions about ownership, exploitation, and benefit distribution. The potential monopolization of space resources by a few powerful corporations or countries could concentrate wealth and deepen inequalities, limiting the global benefits of space resources. To mitigate this risk, many advocate for transparent and equitable frameworks governing space resource use, ensuring that space mining does not merely replicate the socioeconomic disparities seen on Earth. Establishing international guidelines and agreements that prioritize shared access, environmental protection, and ethical oversight will be crucial to balancing exploration with responsibility.

In conclusion, the path to asteroid mining is filled with both technological and moral challenges. The potential for mission failure and technological breakdowns is high, given the demanding conditions and complex operations involved. Meanwhile, the moral and environmental concerns surrounding space mining highlight the need for a balanced approach that prioritizes sustainability, scientific integrity, and equitable access. As asteroid mining technology advances, society will need to address these concerns thoughtfully, ensuring that our expansion into space aligns with values of stewardship and responsibility, minimizing unintended consequences for future generations.

Conclusion

Asteroid mining represents an extraordinary promise for humanity, offering a solution to many of Earth's pressing resource challenges while pushing the boundaries of human capability and vision. The potential to access vast quantities of metals, minerals, and water from space could ease the strain on Earth's ecosystems, support emerging technologies, and provide the foundation for sustainable growth on a global scale. By looking beyond our planet, asteroid mining enables us to envision a future where resource scarcity no longer limits innovation and where humanity can thrive without depleting the natural world that sustains us. This endeavor, with its potential to reshape our economic, environmental, and social landscapes, marks a turning point that could reimagine both Earth's future and our role within the cosmos.

Asteroid mining can be seen as the next evolution of industry—a progression that moves us from extracting resources on Earth to harnessing those in space, embracing a vision of planetary stewardship. For centuries, mining on Earth has fueled economic progress, but it has come at significant environmental cost. Asteroid mining offers a new pathway, one where we access abundant, untouched resources in space, allowing us to conserve and restore Earth's ecosystems. By expanding our reach, we step into a new era of sustainable resource management, one that respects Earth's finite nature while seeking growth in the vast expanses beyond. This shift from terrestrial extraction to space-based resource utilization signals a broader transformation, as humanity evolves from a species bound by planetary limits to one that takes responsibility for the future of both Earth and the space we explore.

As we stand on the threshold of this new frontier, asteroid mining invites us to dream bigger than ever before, to imagine ourselves as pioneers of a world that stretches beyond the familiar boundaries of Earth. This is a future where humans live and work in space, where lunar and Martian colonies become reality, and where interplanetary trade connects distant worlds in a new kind of economy. The vision of an abundant, sustainable future in space is no longer confined to science fiction—it is a possibility within reach, driven by technology, innovation, and imagination. This future beckons to those willing to embrace the challenges and uncertainties of the unknown, daring us to believe in humanity's potential to not only survive but thrive beyond Earth. In dreaming big, we can help to build a legacy that extends far beyond our time, one that redefines what it means to be human and opens up endless possibilities for generations to come.

www.ingramcontent.com/pod-product-compliance
Lightning Source LLC
Chambersburg PA
CBHW071523220526
45472CB00003B/1125